THE EMPTY PILLOW BESIDE YOU

How To Deal With Grief After Losing
Your Life Partner

Joy Fairhall

The Empty Pillow Beside You © Copyright 2020 Joy Fairhall

ISBN: 978-0-6487803-0-4

For more information, email joy@mindbodyjoy.com.au

Dedication

To my husband Graham, deep and beautiful memories of our true love.

To our children Andrew and Katie your Dad would be so proud of you both. I love you more than words can convey.

To Ron who showed me that in pain love can grow again I love you and thank you.

"Death leaves a heartache no one can heal; love leaves a memory no one can steal."

Richard Puz

Table of Contents

CHAPTER 1: Introduction – A Story Of Loss

I held him in my arms watching his breathing as I gently whispered in his ear.

The words were important however not as important as the connection we both craved, we both needed our bodies pressed together giving each other physical presence to hold onto in the dark of the night.

My world was changing, my life, as I knew it, and my husband's, ending. I could hardly breath, I tried to deepen my breathing forcing air into my lungs, lungs that seemed not to want to take the next breath or the next my chest tight.

I willed my husband to do the same. I could hardly breathe, nothing else mattered in those dark quiet moments.

These moments of quiet just the two of us together in love, to breath together, supporting each other as we always had, him in my arms, protecting him on a journey I didn't want him to take.

Holding him gently, whispering my love when all the while my mind and body were screaming. I wanted to hold him tight, to squeeze him in my arms to show my love, instead I held him gently, as gently as the words I continually whispered.

Together in our bed where we had shared our love, conversations and most of all connections it was where we talked from one pillow to the other.

I loved what we called our pillow conversations. I dreaded not having him here beside me, I dreaded the empty pillow beside me if he went.

Our children sleeping in their beds with no idea their hearts would be broken, the very thought bought instant tears to my eyes.

Why were we here, how did we get to this and why so quickly, it's not time - I will not let him go.

Together in those dark quiet moments we faced a vortex, a big black hole of emotions, emotions we both didn't want to face, we were being sucked into it and I fought as much as he fought to stop it.

We both knew, we knew, we didn't want it, we knew there was no choice now however we didn't want to go on this journey alone, we'd always been together and facing this black hole, the vortex alone, no, not alone go away vortex go away black hole we're not ready. Nothing, nothing else was more important than the moments with my love in my arms.

As the time wore on we lay together, I willed him to breath and found myself breathing in the same forced uneven rhythm as he, willing him to take deeper breaths, to stay with me, please stay with me my whole body and mind focused on the same sentences over, over and over, 'please stay with me', 'please stay with us' 'we need you', 'I love you', 'I can't face this alone' over and over and over in my mind.

Yet still the words that I whispered to him were all about our blessings, our life, our memories and most of all our children, our beautiful children who were unknowing, sleeping, so unaware their lives were going to change forever.

'Stay with me', please stay, please....

In a moment, that moment, my arms are empty, my heart the same, I feel like I'm walking in a dream, talking but not speaking, hearing but not understanding, in a dream that's really my nightmare, he's gone, my will to hold onto him with my love wasn't enough, his will to stay weakening, life ebbed slowly from his body until he couldn't hold on anymore.

I had to support him with my love, I had to let him go, he's forever in my heart always in my heart we are connected forever.

I continued whispering into his ear, whispering so his soul hoping his spirit could hear me wanting in that moment for him to once again know how I felt, not wanting to let go, wanting our love and connection to stay entwined forever.

We continued to lay in each other's arms, my love, my husband motionless he lay gone, physically gone, but forever together we are emotionally one.

I couldn't move, if I moved that meant the vortex would start, the big black hole of emotions, he would be physically taken from us, from our home and our lives and I didn't want to move, ever.

In the waiting vortex, I would have to share my loss, the world would intrude and so many things I would have to do that I never wanted to do, I would have to be strong and I didn't feel strong, I didn't want that other side to start, so I lay there quietly holding him almost willing him to give me strength and spiritually guiding him safely into the next world where he would watch over us with his gentle spirit and love us forever.

I gently go to move, my arms heavy from laying in the same position for so long and I felt my heart tearing as I moved my body away from his, the warmth we had felt together gone in an instant and I moved quickly back to where I had been laying not wanting to lose that warmth, not wanting him to feel I had already left his side.

So, hard already, as I feel the suck of that big black hole, the pull of the emotional vortex just waiting.

So hard, the pain of knowing what I had to do, so many things on the list of should and must dos how do I break our precious children's hearts by telling them their precious much-loved Dad had gone?

His parents and brother, my family, my friends, but I keep coming back to our children, oh our poor children, we had protected them from emotional pain their whole life this would break them as it was breaking me.

Their poor hearts they are too young to lose him, they are too young to have to know grief again so soon after their aunty, so hard and the pull of that black vortex and the black hole is getting stronger.

I give myself a few more moments together just us together forever, now physically apart

Laying there I found myself surprised with where my thoughts were going, hardly surprising really as I didn't want them to start focusing on where they should be going and where they would go too soon enough.

I thought about how we spend our lives learning about history, geography, science you name it, we learn about it.

People study for months about an impending birth however we don't study or learn about death.

Why is that so?

This random thought came into my head as I lay there.

Why do we fear death so much?

We often look at the meaning of life but not many learn about the ending, why?

Growing up with a Mum with chronic illness I knew the importance of telling people I loved how special they were to me each and every day.

Friends used to comment on me calling my Mum each and every day, however I knew that one day she might not be there for my call, so it was hugely important to do so each and every day.

Why do we have to make a choice?

Do people have to feel the pain of loss before realizing the need for sharing their love?

Why it is life so much a mix of pleasure and pain?

Oh, and the pain, the pain it was welling in my chest, I had to stop it, I was, I needed to keep it at bay, it had to stay there a little while longer as I lay in my quiet dark world of my emotions.

There is so much more our story, the happy times, the memories, the moment we met, his cheeky smile catching my eye the twinkle and the snap of his fingers in his habitual snap, snap, click he did a habit his children loved, as did I.

The time of our first date, along with birthdays spent laughing and chasing kids, creating memories for them to share together as they grew older and to share with their children, our grandchildren. No, it's not right they have to share them alone without him here.

The camping holidays, the first time we erected our tent, so much laughter and laughter from other campers as we tried our hardest to look like we had done it a hundred times before.

'No, I can't move I can't close the book of your, our life, if I stay quiet the front and back covers won't meet and close, please if I had one wish just one wish…..please, please….

As I lay there I knew, I knew deep within my heart, my very core of my soul that the depth of the pain was there because of the depth of love we had shared.

I had been given a gift, yes it had been physically wrenched away from me however no one could ever take that gift away.

The time we had together, the love, the friendship, the teamwork we had, he was my mate, my husband, my love, physically gone but our gift, the gift of love, memories our children that can never be taken away.

I start to bring some movement into my body moving ever so slightly and I slowly turn my way towards the vortex, the black hole, the turmoil I face it all with tears rolling down along my cheeks for our loss, all the while knowing I had been given such a gift, such a precious gift, the gift of our love.

Knowing with certainty within my broken heart that this was the most precious gift of all.

And so, as I finally take a breath, and another and then another I stretch my fingers to start to bring my own body back to life, to the movement of only one of us breathing, I know this ending is just the beginning.

The book won't ever close….

When I lost my husband at the age of 37, family and friends, who were also grieving and at a loss of what to say or do in their own shock, started sending me books about grief.

Their hearts in the right places; they thought and hoped I would find an answer, advice, a tip or something that would help me get through the days after my heart was literally broken. They were desperate to support us.

I love books and normally I would devour them one after the other, however, one of many overwhelming realities of grief is the total ability to concentrate, it's hard to concentrate on one thing at a time let alone reading a whole book on grief.

The time after death is full and empty at the same time full of things you have to do and don't feel up to doing, people dropping in, funerals to organise, and all the time your heart is screaming go away leave me alone you want people, you don't want people and so it goes on.

When all the things that had to be done were done and people started going back to their normal lives as they should, the emptiness crept in even more so.

Maybe there was something in the books that would help, maybe some advice to show me I wouldn't go mad with grief.

I looked at books that had collected on the table and started to flick through what was now a big pile of books, months down the track, still only able to focus on a paragraph or two, I quickly realised that most of the books were written with a focus on the process of grief, the in's and out and the so called scientific reactions to grief, all very cut and dried as if the author was writing a university paper on just another topic.

Grief is not just another scientific topic to be explained from A to Z. Grief is full of overwhelming emotions, physical and emotional, it's full of dark and light and it's totally not relatable to any life experience you've ever had before.

It's hard to relate the depth of grief to anyone else unless they've been immersed in grief before.

You feel broken hearted, lost, overwhelmed and feeling like you've been sucked into a vortex of the unknown swirling and coiling around you day in and day out.

You wonder if you will ever smile and be happy let alone feel Joy ever again.

This is why the books I was given gave me no answers there was such a disconnect between what was written on those pages to what I was feeling and experiencing.

The way the information was shared was almost like a daily checklist start here and end here and you'll be good to get on with life. Really?

The books were so totally unrelatable to what my family, my beautiful children who had lost their world - their Dad, and I were going through.

Where were the books that spoke the language of grief, my grief for my husband and as a Mum who now had to process her own grief as well as support her children, where were those books?

Where were the books that when you picked them up your instinctively knew the author understood you and what you were going through?

I found literally zero books that spoke this language that I was able to understand, that gave me information in a way that my cloudy befuddled mind could focus on for a brief millisecond or so.

I was all over the place and found these books, the order of the book, was not how I was processing grief at all.

That's when I decided I would write a book myself and here now in this quiet moment you're holding a book that speaks the real language of grief, a language you wish you never needed to learn, a book about all that encompasses the reality of grief, the real grief warts and all.

In this book I openly share my emotions, feelings and thoughts to truly connect, support and share on a deeply personal level.

I support you from all I've learned personally and professionally in a realistic and non-sterile way sharing with you useful, not useless, advice on dealing with daily life now and in the future.

This book can be read in any order because that's what grief is like, you don't follow a standard list, you may find yourself needing the end chapter first and vice versa and that's ok.

This little book is my hand reaching out to support you and your very real grief concerns and questions.

Things like first anniversaries, family gatherings, dumb things people say, triggers that set you off and even crying in the middle of a supermarket aisle.

The missed conversations with your partner as you lay in bed with the empty pillow beside.

Included is guidance for that practical stuff you have to do even though you want to just run and hide.

Guidance for moments straight after your loss, notifying banks, car registration and more, everything simple and straight forward so you can understand it through your fog of grief.

To truly connect with you I bare my soul and share my story.

This book is here to love, support you and guide you as if I'm standing right beside you.

Written because I've been, where you are now, and I understand.

CARE POINT - Grief is such a personal topic and normally when I see people, I would be able to see you to gauge your reactions and personally support you if you feel overwhelmed. However this is a book and I can't see you to be aware of your emotions and possible reaction to things I may cover.

Therefore, throughout my book you'll find what I call *'Care Points'*.

Care Points are little pointers that I would normally share in person should you feel confused, upset or more.

So, before we begin, I ask you to please acknowledge your feelings, know they are there, observe them and let them go. If tears come as you read let them come, if anger arises grab a pillow and punch it, if you feel overwhelmed stop reading and go for a short walk even into the backyard just walk.

All these reactions are ok, and I'll still be here when you return.

In Chapter Seven under Tips and Tools I have a quick method I've developed that you can do if you experience any anxiety or overwhelm it's called '3 Minutes to Calm'™ it's there to support you and calm you so you can take in, without overwhelm, what you need from this book.

If you need personal support my contact details are in the back of this book, call for support if it all becomes too much.

Now I feel I have supported you as best as I can, here through the pages of my book, let's move onto supporting you further through the rest of my book.

CHAPTER 2: What Is Grief –

What You Need To Know

Grief is such an emotional time and the reality that death is a normal part of everyone's life just doesn't relate to us right now, how can so much pain be normal?

If we've never personally been touched by loss how do we know what lies after it?

For most of us death is to be feared and something we don't openly talk about. No wonder we don't understand what's normal and if there is a normal at all.

During this time of grief, you'll often feel vulnerable and alone even if surrounded by a room full of people.

Take a breath, know that you will get through this and understanding more about grief and what is to come will give you a little more control and understanding during a time when control and understanding seems to have flown right out the window.

Here, in this chapter, I share the reality, mixed in with the official definition and also a little of the psychology behind grief. It's important to know these, so you can understand grief on different levels and also to understand why everyone feels and reacts differently.

I share what you want to know right now, what to expect, why you feel the way you do to coping with the reactions of others and lastly common myths, that seem to be widely are accepted as truth, when in fact they are most definitely not.

What Is Grief

Grief is defined as 'a normal emotional response to loss'.

Grief is 'intense sorrow caused by someone's death, a familiar pattern or situation in life such as the loss of a pet, a broken relationship or a future loss through work change or even a serious illness diagnosis'.

In your quest to find help with your grief, you may have come across some 'quick fixes' offered over the Internet, however sadly, there is no 'quick fix' for grief.

However, there are effective and comfortable ways to help soothe your broken heart and ease you gently back into your life.

In your search on the internet you would inevitably come across reference to '5 or 7 stages of grief' that are seemingly the 'right 'way to grieve they have been used as a grief checklist of sorts.

Elizabeth Kubler-Ross author of these books and guides did have a positive effect on releasing her book as it did open up more conversation about grief.

However, what is not well known is that Kubler-Ross developed the 'stages' that are listed in her book to describe the process patients go through as they come to terms with a terminal illness's diagnosis, not in fact for grief at all.

In saying that, grief can definitely be a part of being diagnosed with a life ending illness, I see clients for this type of grief as well, however it doesn't go through the same stages identically as when you lose a loved one.

Studies* have shown that when your grieving you don't usually progress through defined stages in any particular order checking one off before moving to the next and the next.

However, this is what is seen as truth in the eyes of the wider communities however it really is just one big myth

The Most Believed 7 Stages of Grief

- Shock
- Denial
- Guilt
- Anger & bargaining
- 'Depression', reflection, loneliness
- Reconstruction & working through
- Acceptance

Kates story

When Kate lost her sister after a long illness, she thought she would cope with her sister's loss as she, as she stated, "was prepared and glad she wasn't suffering any more". Kate came to me when she found she as struggling she'd found other people just didn't understand. She felt like she wasn't grieving normally, and something was really wrong with her.

She asked me if I could 'cure' her of her grief because it hurt so much. I explained to her that what she was feeling was normal and she wasn't ill or abnormal at all. Tough to hear when you're in so much pain but this is what she needed to hear.

Once she realised that feeling relieved and sad at the same time was normal, she felt heard and less conflicted and more at ease with her grief.

There is no right way or wrong way to experience grief you might experience grief one way and your friend might experience it in a completely different way.

Please don't compare yourself to others, as I've mentioned before, and definitely don't beat yourself up if you're not going through the 'stages' in order.

What is not often shared about grief is the intense emotional and physical reaction you experience following the loss of your loved one.

Grief is not only about deep sadness but also the loss of a loved one can bring anguish, loneliness and can feel like the most awful debilitating emotion ever felt.

When someone you love dies your life changes forever from that very moment, they leave your life and it is this the deep intense emotional and physical reaction that confuses because you've never felt this anguish before.

I personally feel that the definition of grief should include "the feeling of reaching out for someone, who's always been there, only to discover they are no longer there and feeling the huge emptiness in their place."

All emotions aside the emptiness that comes from wanting to talk to the person who you shared your life with just tears your heart to pieces.

What to Expect

To be truthfully honest expect a roller coaster from the overwhelming emotions to actual physical reactions.

A roller coaster was exactly what it felt like to me day in day out in the beginning. Ups and downs as I barrelled or coasted along this grief ride of emotions and the totally unexpected physical reactions that I'd never heard about before.

What I didn't realise was that grief would be so complex, far more complex, than I'd expected. I had believed that grief was just sadness and emptiness and what I personally found was it was so much more.

Grief is like nothing you've ever felt before no matter how prepared you think you are, in short grief is unique.

When I lost my husband, I thought I would move through grief sort of like a checklist after all that was what was talked about the most 5 stages one, two, three, four, five easy right?

A checklist that I could, once I got through it, meant I'd soon be living a normal life once more, how wrong I was, life never returns to my normal, what it did do was morph into a new normal instead.

Grief is very different for everyone and while you might go through the supposed normal reactions you might not, on the other hand experience them all.

In fact, as I mentioned above regrading stages of grief, one of the most misunderstood myths about grief is that we all grieve the same way.

This is the furthest thing from the truth. Grief is such an individual experience and how you grieve, or how you choose to grieve, depends on many things which I'll cover as we go along.

This is why no two people will react the same way to the same loss and one of the most important things to remember when your grieving, is not to compare yourself to others.

I've had clients come to me and say I'm not grieving 'normally' because they're constantly comparing themselves to others and, as you'll see as we move through this book, there are reasons why the depth of grief varies so much.

No one has lived your life to this very second of your life, no one understands the loss of your loved one, no one can understand the depth of your love and relationship and no one has lived your life up to now, when you were together, you simply cannot compare yourself to someone else.

You may experience overwhelm in general as well as overwhelming tiredness and fogginess.

Taking in information and understanding written information seems beyond you at times and if someone asks you to 'make a decision', well what was easy before is now like walking backwards up Mt Everest.

In fact, it's a scientifically tested fact that when you're grieving it can take you up to six seconds longer to process information.

You'll have times you want to be surrounded by people and others when inside your head you're screaming to be alone.

You will cry in a way you've never cried before, deep gut wrenching, stomach hurting, primal crying, the depth of which surprised me when I lost my husband.

It was not only the emotional and physical reaction to the loss of my loved husband, it was the depth of my loss, my mind and bodies reaction to my loss that overtook me no matter how hard I tried to be in control, there seems to be nothing that ever really prepares you for that response.

The mind and body are intrinsically linked and so below I share a few emotional and physical reactions you may experience.

You'll see I've also included spirituality or religion as this is often missed when talking about responding to grief.

Depending on your faith and beliefs your beliefs may bring you much comfort or it may challenge your beliefs and bring about a total opposite reaction.

There are many words to describe the emotions we feel when grieving, I won't list them all here, however it's important to know that often we can't even begin to describe the feeling and emotions consuming your life since the loss of your loved one.

Some of the common emotional reactions can include:

- Intense sadness
- Shock
- Despair
- Worry about the future
- Anger
- Confusion
- Guilt
- Empty
- Relief

Client story

A client, whose husband had passed away only 8 months ago, came to me because they she was feeling like she wasn't grieving properly. She said to me "It's been eight months now why do I still feel like it was yesterday?" "Why do I still feel like I'm walking in a dream each and every day?"

My answer to her questions was that she was grieving exactly as she needs to; everyone grieves their own way. This particular client had also been with her loved one since she was 16 and she was 82 when she lost him, it was no wonder she felt a profound sense of loss and grief.

This list is not the be all and end all of the emotions I have documented all the word's and ways my clients have used to describe grief and I'm sure the way you feel right now you would find that on the list I have.

I have created a list of common emotional and physical responses which you can find in chapter six.

While you may have been expecting the sad emotions, I bet you are as surprised, as I was back when I lost my husband, by the physical reactions to grief you are experiencing as well.

When you think about it grief is a major stress on your mind and body, one of the biggest in fact that you will experience in your lifetime, and, of course, stress affects the body, mentally and physically.

It just hadn't entered my mind that I would not only have to cope with emotional reactions, but I would also be physically affected as well.

By knowing and understanding this you will be in a slightly better place than I was back then.

Some of the common physical reactions experienced in grief are listed below

- Crying
- Nausea
- Headaches
- Insomnia
- Loss of appetite
- Stomach upsets
- Restlessness
- Jaw soreness
- Shoulder tension

Again, there are more physical reactions than those I've listed above however these are the most common.

Grief

It's ok to need a
guiding hand

Mind Body Joy

Common Spiritual Reactions to Grief:

- Feeling comforted by your faith
- Feeling abandoned or punished by your God/ Universe/Higher being (whoever you follow in your faith)
- Questioning your religious/spiritual beliefs

- Feeling spiritually connected to the person who died
- Needing to receive forgiveness
- Finding hope in prayer/spiritual beliefs
- Finding new purpose in life

Why You Feel the Way You Do

I've mentioned before that grief is unique and a highly individual experience and there are many reasons why we can't all be lumped into one grief file together.

No one has lived your life, your values, your spirituality, your life experiences and all of these moments, right up to this very moment, play an important part into how you grieve.

As a result of grief being individual, it is also unique to each person, in other words, the intensity of how someone grieves directly correlates to the uniqueness of their relationship.

The Grief Reactions of Others

The reactions of others to the loss of your loved one either as a family member, friend or even work colleagues, will also vary.

You may find yourself surprised by the depth of another people's grief to your loved one's loss. There may be people who you personally may have thought might not be affected who very much are affected.

Other times you may find yourself wondering if a person really cared for your loved as much as they say they do, when they don't share any emotions at all.

Again, we don't know how we will react until we are faced with a loss of someone we care about, they maybe as surprised as you by their reactions.

In cases where you find yourself getting aggravated or even angry with someone because it looks like they don't care, bear in mind that they might be hiding their emotions from you to protect you so you don't take time to sooth them in their grief when they feel it's you who should be cared for.

They may prefer to grieve away from prying eyes or behind closed doors so as not to upset you further.

My advice here is to let things go, you have enough on your plate to be worried, angry or upset by other people's emotions or lack thereof.

7 Myths You Need To Know Are Not Real

There are seven myths around grief that are commonly believed are true and factual without any proof to show they are true.

Myths are exactly that, things that people have shared, that are then believed and then seemingly become truth and shared as such.

I know these myths were a part of what I was taught and believed over the years of my childhood and into adulthood.

I guess I never really thought about where they came from and in fact if they were true, they just were what was commonly associated with grief.

When I was going through my own grief, I realized that these 'facts', these myths were in fact more like urban legend stories that had been told without any science behind them at all.

Give It Time

You don't and won't miss someone any less even if you lost them years and years ago. Grief becomes a bit more bearable and less painful as time goes on but does hurt any less? Do they really expect we will miss them any less in time? No.

I still remember the loss of my husband in 1997 as if they were yesterday. Time has, in my words, softened my grief; I still miss him, I still grieve for him as do our children, those wounds and the loss is a part of me and always will be.

Giving grief more time certainly won't change how I feel about losing the person I loved, and it won't for you either.

The emotions and reaction ease and soften in time but the loss of your loved one stays with you forever, it's how you choose to remember those times that is important.

Be Strong

As the daughter of a sick Mum I heard this statement throughout my entire life from Dad, "You have to be strong for your Mum", or from others "Joy you're so strong looking after your Mum", I took this literally and became the strong one in the family even to this day.

Taking on things for my family when I was in fact the one that needed support as a child. What I found was that being strong and not giving into my emotions wasn't healthy at all.

It hurt me emotionally and physically because I wasn't expressing my sadness or my tiredness or asking for help when I myself when I needed it.

Being strong sets the wrong example and puts so much pressure on the person we are giving our expectations too and can often bring more heartache.

Telling someone to be strong goes against releasing emotions and may lead to ongoing challenges.

Grief is Private

Society has taught us not to burden others with our grief. Grieving alone in private can be a good thing however you need to have a balance.

By being alone we can acknowledge our true feelings and start to sort things out in our mind as we come to live with our loss, without other people telling you what you should and shouldn't be feeling or doing.

However, if you start finding yourself wanting to be alone for longer and longer periods and the sadness is overtaking your life that's when you may need to seek professional support.

On the other hand, some people may also feel they can't support you as they really want to, as they might feel they don't want to intrude on your grief.

I felt that way after I lost two close colleagues at work. I didn't want to bother anyone with my sadness, so I stayed to myself as I felt I had no right to intrude on the family during their grief even though I wanted to drop in and let them know I felt their loss and was missing their loved ones as well.

Often, we find that those who have lost someone and are grieving actually love hearing stories of their loved one and if you share about time you spent together whether it was socially or through a workplace it certainly brings them back to happier times and for them makes their loved ones life even more special and makes them happy.

So my advice on this, at times, tricky subject is to send a message to the family and offer to sit with them for a cuppa and let them know you'd like to share a conversation about how wonderful or special or whatever your relationship was with their loved one.

If they choose to and if they're up to it, and please let the family choose what they would like to do. At least you have reached out to them and you never know down the track they might seek you out for a cuppa when they are ready.

Don't Show Sad Emotions

I often ponder that as babies, we were free to express our emotions with no expectation at all. We laughed when we were happy and cried when we were sad.

Our emotions could change at the drop of a hat it was expected and accepted behaviour. But at some point, in our childhood, an invisible switch was flipped, and we were told now we were 'big' boys or girls it suddenly was no longer 'acceptable' to freely express our emotions.

We were told "Big girls don't cry" or "Man up boy you're a man now you shouldn't be crying".

In all the research and psychology available it has been shown, in fact proven, that when we acknowledge our feelings when we can process them better and let them go, we heal and are able to get them through them in an easier and effective way.

 It doesn't mean that they don't still hurt, they do, however letting them go helps, it truly does.

In Time You'll Find Love Again

Many of us were probably told after a relationship break-up "Don't feel bad, there are plenty of fish in the sea". Funnily enough I had a few people say to me not long after I lost my husband "You're young you'll find love again".

I was simply floored! I couldn't even contemplate feeling happy ever again, let alone falling in love again and how dare they think I could love someone ever again?

I kept telling people I'd had the love of my life I didn't need anyone else ever again.

Statements such as these don't help us to feel any better and it implies in reality that we shouldn't be grieving as deeply, as we are, as we have a future love waiting in the wings.

We may have or may not in the future no one knows however when you have just lost the love of your life being told this is certainly no help at all and should never be uttered to anyone no matter what age.

Keep Yourself Busy

Speaking from experience I can say I became a busy-aholic after the loss of my husband. I thought if I kept myself and my kids busy enough, my kids' grief would ease, and they would cope a little easier.

But it never did, it just got buried. Consequently, it churned and churned for us all until it showed up in my daughter when she began having panic attacks.

You may ask did she grieve and yes, she did, did she share her feeling yes, she did but not at the depth she should have. How could she?

She had a Mum who had shown her all her life that you had to be strong, to care for others no matter what, so, that's what she did for me.

She was trying with all her might to stay strong for me, to be strong so I wouldn't worry about her and her brother.

All the while I felt like I was going to explode with being strong!

I became exhausted emotionally, physically and spiritually and keeping busy was just an avoidance technique and can be one of the worst ways to handle grief.

Of course, there is being busy for emotional avoidance and being busy in a healing way, it's definitely a fine line.

Let me explain, when I lost my husband, we were just about to demolish half our house and build a long-awaited extension which were going to build ourselves.

We always renovated together, and we were excited to start our biggest adventure yet, the plans were drafted and ready, the permits done and we were good to go.

Alas the loss of my husband put this huge lifelong project on the back burner well and truly.

However, as it was a such a dream of his it became the project my children and I could focus on as we built our new life together as a family of three.

The plans were slightly changed, we now couldn't afford the size of the initial extension, and we started the project in honour of my children's dad and my love, my husband.

It kept us busy and it kept us together as we shared many conversations about how Dad would do it this way and how Dad would have had his green overalls on and a hole in one knee already, so many conversations shared over plaster board and dust.

We spoke of their Dad and often, we kept the conversations open and together we built the extension and finished the project their Dad had wanted as we built our life together slowly without him physically there.

Now I'm not suggesting you demolish half your house as a way of healing, however a project or plan that allows you all to talk about your loved one is a great way to start conversations, to talk openly about your loved one, to share tears and laughter together and start building a new life without them, without feeling like your forgetting them.

Knowing about what grief is and how you and others will react will give you a bit of forewarning for the days ahead and once again, remember that what you are feeling is normal.

Take the pressure off yourself, understand that you need time, support, time with people and time alone and take or do anything else you might need to get through this truly awful period of your life.

CARE & ACTIONS

Care

- Know at all times that what you are experiencing is normal - even when it doesn't feel like it

- Let your emotions go don't try to hold them back, let them go trust me you'll feel better

- Talk to your friends or family if you need too - don't try to be strong

- Seeking support early really helps

Actions

- If you find yourself reacting to how others feel grab a notebook and write down your feelings

- Be yourself, no one knows how you grieve behind closed doors, so let it go with others

- Buy a notebook or a journal and write down any thoughts constantly swirling through your head it will help clear them and then you can work on them at a later date

* https://www.scientificamerican.com/article/five-fallacies-of-grief/

CHAPTER 3: The First Few Minutes, Hours And 6 Months – How To Survive

No matter how much notice we are given we're never fully prepared for the reality of the losing a loved one.

We're all different and every person, every relationship, every circumstance, every belief will form and contribute to form your own unique grief experience.

You may feel emotions that surprise you and shock you, you may feel calm and accepting to fully losing control or you may feel completely numb, it's all normal so put aside any preconceived thoughts about what you were expecting.

When someone you love passes away don't be rushed in those moments after they have gone to start the next step.

Take the time to be alone, if you choose to, to talk to them, care for them, dress or bathe them or simply hold them.

If you choose and you feel comfortable to do so you may also consider others to do the same.

There is no hurry for you to be separated from your loved one immediately of course everything you choose to do in those first few moments need to be comfortable for you.

There is no urgent rush for your loved one to be taken away from you whether they are in hospital or home again you choose what is comfortable to you.

When my loved husband passed away at home, I notified the doctor and then spent many hours with him privately and then I faced the most awful moment the moment I had to tell my children that their beloved Dad had gone.

I then rang my husband's parents and my parents knowing they would come over immediately.

In our own quiet and private time and space I gave my children the choice of whether they wanted to see their father or not.

I must stress here that the option of seeing a loved one who is a parent who has passed can affect children in very different ways and can cause trauma and shock and needs to be handled very carefully.

I can't advise you in this book if this is right for your children only you as the surviving parent will know if this is advisable. I professionally cannot advise you either way without knowing your children and yourself, the situation and so much more.

Every child is different, and their ages of course comes into it as well.

Our families arrived and spent time with my husband and friends some of whom chose to go into our room and say goodbye.

I felt it was important that they could pay their own tributes in private. Of course, not everyone chooses to do this and again the choice is yours, you may not feel in control at this time but please take control of this situation don't do anything or let others do anything you don't feel comfortable with.

So, as a reminder the first few minutes and hours are completely in your control even though your world has fallen apart and the weeks and months that follow will be one of your life's hardest challenges.

Six months, wow, I remember getting to six months after the loss of my loved husband and thinking where did that time go?

It had gone by super-fast and yet on the other hand each day had felt like it was passing ever so slowly like a movie in slow motion, how could both be feelings be possible?

I'd lost days or I couldn't remember them, my memory of that time was foggy, I pretty much just 'existed' I was literally on auto pilot.

If it was night time I cleaned my teeth and went to bed, the sun rose, I got up, it was routine that got me through, as with any routine I didn't have to think about anything it was just rote.

Of course, during that time, I had things I had to do, some I wished I didn't have to do, my husband's farewell, supporting my children who were so lost and broken and not to mention all the paperwork!

I managed, however I'm really not sure how. There was so much paperwork and I wondered why there was such an expectation that you have to complete all the required legal paperwork, when your head is mush, it still leaves me shaking my head from side to side.

In this chapter I share information about what you need to do and other things that can simply wait, this chapter will guide you along the first six months and support you along the way.

The Farewell Of Your Husband & Things You Have To Do

When your loved one passes, the last thing you want to think about is paperwork. Keeping family and friends close around you, working through the shock of how hard grief actually is and taking care of your emotional needs can seem like the only important things worth addressing in the days, and even weeks after losing someone close to you.

That's why tasks such as handling bills, dealing with a funeral home, finding bank accounts and so much more can take you by surprise.

It seems ridiculous that at a time when you are the most stressed and emotional you'll ever be in your life is the time you need to make these plans and handle important paperwork, however with that said legally there are things that you can't ignore.

If you've already had your organised wills and had a funeral plan in place it makes things so much simpler and some of the paperwork will be reduced.

Again, I ponder that we are so organised and prepared, for the birth of a new life, we literally have nine months of planning, but for our own deaths we often don't give it a thought.

We plan and prepare for a new baby and their birth
So why don't we plan and prepare for our own death?

Please don't let others take control of things you may already have discussed with your loved one, if you want something for the funeral make sure you're wishes are heard.

If you have children, young or older, ask them how they would like to be involved and listen to their wishes, don't push them to do things you feel they 'should' be doing let their words guide you.

I've created a simple and easy guideline with suggestions and a checklist for planning the farewell of your loved one, you'll find it in chapter six.

Use this as guide to make sure you understand your choices, also included are important tasks that need to be done and why they need to be done in the early days after your loss.

This is the time to start delegating things that need to be done to close family or trusted friends.

It might be hard, and you might feel you need to do it all yourself, but trust me delegation is the way to go if you can.

During this time, you will feel utterly tired, so delegation really supports you and leaves only the very important tasks for you to manage.

Give your death notices to a friend or the funeral home to organise, ask a friend to purchase you some tea/coffee supplies and biscuits for those who will drop in to see you.

Assign one family member to be the main point of contact who can take all the calls asking how you are, what the funeral plans are and so on.

Having someone take your calls means taking some of the pressure off you and means that you don't need to keep explaining the same information over and over to many concerned friends.

Delegating certainly takes some of the pressure off managing day today tasks and reduces some of the day to day stress, reduces your workload and leaves you far less exhausted.

Certificate Of Death

When someone passes, a doctor or medical professional has to pronounce them dead in order for the process to move forward.

If someone dies in a hospital or a nursing home, the staff on hand provide that service. When someone dies, a doctor must sign a certificate that confirms the death.

Funeral arrangements can't be made until the doctor has signed and issued this certificate called a 'Doctor's Certificate of Cause of Death'. The funeral company can then take the deceased into their care.

If you are using a funeral home for the farewell the funeral director will collect all the information needed to register the death. They'll send this to the birth, deaths and marriages registry in your state or territory.

If I Should Go – Unknown author

If I should go tomorrow

It would never be goodbye,

For I have left my heart with you,

So, don't you ever cry.

Inform Friends And Family

Informing family, friends, and acquaintances to let them know your loved one has gone is tough.

It's exhausting and emotional and often when you feel ok to call someone you find as soon as they pick up the phone and hear their voice the tears come and choke your words.

Sharing such sad news is hard, so only call those you feel you personally need to inform and let someone else close to you call the others, again delegate where possible.

Making Farewell Arrangements

Not everyone wants or has a funeral there are many options available for farewells these days.

However, you say farewell there is usually a gathering to share in the farewell of your loved one.

How, you choose to say farewell is completely up to you, that is unless your loved one left specific arrangement in their will and in that case, you need to follow their specific wishes.

Farewells can be in the form of a traditional funeral or a memorial, it can be a gathering of people at your home or other venue or even sprinkling your loved one's ashes somewhere special or burying them in a special place.

All of these are ways of saying farewell and goodbye to the physical presence of your loved one.

However, remember how you choose to say farewell know that it is their physical presence you are saying goodbye too, not the emotional love you have for each other.

If you already have a funeral home picked out you can call the funeral home directly and they will take over the arrangements from picking up and looking after your loved one from where they have passed and providing support about the planning the funeral, notices, date and time of the farewell and even more.

They will contact you to meet face to face to finalise and organise the farewell as per your wishes.

I found that having those you love, and those who may be involved in the farewell around you during this meeting not only supports you it also gives everyone a chance to share and participate in planning the final farewell.

You may like to choose songs and photos to be played or decorate the service venue with your loved one's favourite colours, posters of their favourite sport team or even photos of the family.

The farewell is what you want and so it's important you share and make these inclusions as you discuss the arrangements with the funeral home.

For my husband's funeral we had a Ford car racing flag, that my Mum had called and organised for, on his coffin along with other items the children had chosen. The flag now hangs proudly in remembrance of their Dad in his shed where he loved pottering around and watching the Ford cars racing.

Funerals don't have to be sad events, when I held my mother's funeral, we held it on her birthday, which some people found odd I might add, however it seemed fitting we farewelled her on the day she was born 80 odd years ago when the world was blessed with her birth.

Her grandchildren and great-grandchildren quietly lit a birthday candle before the ceremony marking the occasion as Mum had always loved birthdays and they didn't want her to miss out on her birthday candles, that was their special way of showing they cared for and loved her.

Mums photo montage, which is usually accompanied by sad songs, was set to happy music, a melody of Doris Day songs that were bright and melodic which made everyone smile and had their toes tapping and hands clapping along.

It was the celebration of life I wanted for my Mum as she was known for her love of music and song and making people happy. She would have loved it.

I also provided a memory jar where people could write their special memory of Mum, this helped family and friends recall special times they had shared with Mum after the funeral and we as a family loved sharing these memories on the first Christmas without Mum.

Reading the stories and memories of her friends, some we had never even heard before, made us smile and it felt really special to know that Mum had touched so many people's lives.

I have shared this idea with many of my clients and they all love it.

When you receive the official death certificate it's important to make multiple copies, as you'll need them.

You'll need copies for bereavement leave from your workplace, as will your family members for their leave. Be aware that when you are closing bank accounts etc you'll need to show them the original certificate, so make sure you keep it in a place where you won't lose it.

The importance of having the original available wasn't explained to me at the time of losing my husband and I found myself having to re book appointments at financial institutions as I'd only taken a copy rather than the original.

Be aware of the costs of farewells, even with a simple straightforward cremation or funeral the cost can escalate into the thousands so be prepared.

If you have an attorney handling your loved ones will, they can assist you with the payment from the estate at a later date.

Clients Story

My husband was a mad motorcycle and Harley Davidson man, so it seemed only fitting I organised a motorbike funeral for him. I found a company that actually carried the coffin to the venue and then to the cemetery. I felt that I was giving my husband a very special last gift, and I know he would have loved it.

The Will And Executor

The will of your loved one is a legal document that informs surviving family members of their last wishes and how they want their belongings such as money, property, memorabilia etc will go after their death.

The Executor of the Will is responsible for distributing the person's assets as per your loved ones wishes to the people named in the Will. All the assets will be distributed after all debts, if any, are paid

The will may need to go through a process known as probate, legal execution of a will, which helps transfer property over to any heirs.

If you and your loved one jointly owned property or estate probate may not be required. This is where the assistance of an expert really assists and supports you.

Wills sometime include instructions for their farewell so even if you have discussed with your loved one their wishes for their farewell plans make sure you read their will just in case, they have added anything that you may not be aware of.

Money And Assets

When someone passes you are legally required to notify any financial institutions. If you need access to your loved one's account for funeral and other expenses, contact the financial institution and they can assist. If you hold joint accounts, it makes it easier to access however be aware that releasing funds differs from bank to bank.

Unexpected costs can often come due in the period after a death and can lead to shock about how you are going to handle it all.

If you have a cosignatory, joint account, the account may still be able to be accessed, or it may have to be handled and settled with the help of your attorney. If you find that medical bills and other bills are piling up call the support line and inform them of your loss as most companies extend the time to pay in these situations.

I found that having an attorney really helped when I recently lost my mother, they handled all the bills, I simply had to send them to my contact, and they paid them from mums' estate.

To be totally honest, I was too stubborn, pretending to be strong, when I lost my husband and did everything myself and found it absolutely exhausting.

I went to the banks, transferred car registrations, cancelled insurance you name it I did it, it simply didn't occur to me that someone else could do it.

Looking back, I wished I 'd delegated most of that as I found it really tiring, physically and emotionally.

Going to these paperwork-based businesses and informing them about losing my husband and hearing the same jaded platitudes and seeing them holding his certificate of death as if it was just another piece of paper was terribly difficult.

What They Won't Tell You About Loss

I mentioned in the previous chapter that one of the surprising things I found was the tiredness and inability to focus.

As someone who is normally very organised and capable it was a shock to feel that I could hardly focus on opening and reading a letter without feeling exhausted and being unable to take in what I'd just read.

It was especially hard as I was very aware that my young children were suffering, and I needed to be there for them, especially as all I wanted to do was hold them tight and heal their broken hearts.

As heartbreaking as it was to lose the love of my life it was even more heartbreaking to see my children suffering.

I found myself trying to be strong for them and my tears would come when they were asleep in bed, as I held a photo of him close to my heart deep gut wrenching sobs rose deep from my stomach that tore through my body and out through my mouth, I've never heard such noises before and they were coming from my heart and oh how it hurt not to have my husband by my side, it was emotionally and physically exhausting.

Time away is often not considered when you lose someone however, it is something that I suggest as being very helpful. The time I spent with my kids on a week away after the funeral was especially healing and gentle and soothing.

We were away from phones, people dropping in and away from those beautiful but sad and concerned faces around us.

This sounds especially selfish doesn't it?

However, putting yourself first is absolutely not selfish, it is needed. If there had been grief retreats for families when I lost my husband, I would have been there with my kids in a flash.

It's the reason why I now run my own grief retreats for those who need them. It's comforting to know you can be nurtured without being fussed over, nice to be given tools and techniques that will support you over the coming trying year and beyond.

So, my advice is taking yourself away even for a weekend when you can and investigate if there are retreats in your area that specialise in grief retreats and support.

Another thing I'd like to share and something that I found interesting, personally, was how I felt when I found myself laughing.

Not that I laughed much in the first few months but when I did it was usually as we were recollecting a beautiful and funny memory of my husband or the kids of their Dad.

As the laughter burst from my lips, I felt guilt! Yes, guilt how could I laugh so soon after losing my love.

We shouldn't feel guilty for laughing in fact looking back and remembering things in a positive way helps your heart heal.

It's nice to feel the rush of happy moments after the tears. So, if you can find ways to look back and find those funny memories do it, trust me you'll feel so much better.

Research shows that laughter releases dopamine, the happy hormone, and this certainly helps release stress and relax your body at a time when stress has seemingly become your best friend.

What To Focus On Right Now?

To be honest focus on only what has to be done and that's it.

Don't try and get everything done in the first few weeks.

Do the legal stuff when you have to, make your farewell special take your time with the arrangements it truly helps those left behind.

If you want to share your feelings and love but feel you can't stand up in front of everyone write what you want to say and give it to a family member or trusted friend to read your letter for you on the day.

Focus on acknowledging your feelings, I know I keeps saying this but it's really important to do so.

Focus on one day at a time, don't go trying to plan for months ahead right now, it will tire you even more than you need.

Now is not the time to decide on big decisions when your mind is foggy, and your decisions clouded by emotions life altering decisions should not be made in the first twelve months. This is not the time to think about selling your home or other large decisions.

As a person who normally loved paperwork, I hated it, firstly because my brain had to use so much effort to read and take in what I had to do and more importantly I had to continually write or tick the box that stated my status as widow.

I personally dislike the word widow and widow at the age of 37 just didn't compute with my mind and seeing it there right in front of me with every form I had to complete really irked me!

Being continually asked "Are you the widow" was very hard I know officially that's what I was but, in my mind, I'm was still a wife, his wife and still am his wife forever more.

I didn't divorce him, we still loved each other greatly why does that change just because I'd lost him in this life?

For some taking off your wedding ring is something you feel you need to do, for me I still wear my wedding ring along with new rings in memory of the marriage we shared.

Of course, there is more to come and things still to be done but this chapter is all about what has to be done fairly quickly from a personal and legal viewpoint.

There is a logical way forward when somebody passes even though it doesn't feel that way right now.

Allow yourself to be assisted by the specialists who can help you with the funeral arrangements, immediate finances, family and legal requirements and the caring of your loved one until the farewell. Enlist and accept support of your family and close friends.

Numbness and shock are natural in the first few days and weeks and, as I said before, don't be surprised by any emotion you feel, they are normal.

You will have to deal with many emotions and a number of decisions please take one step at a time and understand you will not always feel this way.

Devote your energies to what is important to you and your family, use this time to create a meaningful tribute and farewell for your loved one as doing this is a family is also a way to support each other and a beginning of starting a beautiful memory of your lives together.

I Know – Joy Fairhall

I know tears will be shed, now that they are gone, but smiles should be given for the life they lived

I know the memories you created together will stand you in good stead

I know you will close your eyes and pray for them to be back in your arms, but please open your eyes and see all that they have left

I know your heart feels empty, but notice as well how it's full of love from all they shared

I know the empty pillow beside you is the reminder they're not there

I know that you'll smile in the years ahead in memory of the conversations you shared

I know you feel you can't face tomorrow but remember the joy of yesterdays and live today for all the yesterdays they shared with you

I know you only see now the gap they've left, but please remember how full the life that you shared

I know you can choose to be closed to tomorrows, living your life always looking back

I know it hurts to live today

I know that you can choose instead to see the life and love and laughter you shared

I know, as you know deep in your heart, that you can choose to do what they really want for you,

I know they want you to go on and truly live your life

I know they would want you to open your eyes, smile, feel their love fill your heart and cherish all you shared

I know they want you to live your life remembering with love yesterday and creating new memories for tomorrow

I know you can,

I know you can

CARE & ACTIONS

Care

- Delegate, delegate, delegate things to others to remove some of your stress – you don't have to do it all

- Think of your family and friends and their unique ways they can support you. Who can you call in the early hours, who makes you laugh etc?

- Rest as you need to and don't worry if your sleep patterns are all out of whack - you need rest

- Be you - let the emotions come and go cry if you need to cry, vent if you need to rant don't analyse it all just go with the flow.

Actions

During this time overwhelm can creep up on you in an instant

- Learn to say no and STOP.

- STOP take time out, even for a few minutes.

- If you feel like the information being shared with you is not sinking in tell the person who is sharing the information to STOP and go slower.

- STOP taking on other people's expectations of how you grieve and grieve the way you feel.

- STOP and take time away

CHAPTER 4: Grief In Reality –

Now And The Future

In the previous chapters I've explained what grief is, how to listen and be guided by your own emotions and feelings, and I've also explained how the 5 stages of grief were actually created to guide those diagnosed with chronic illness as well as how grief is simply not a list of stages you tick off until you start living a magical 'happy ever' after life.

Grief flows between one emotion to another and sometimes back again. It would be so much simpler if grief did follow an easy to read map, but the reality is different.

The many diagrams you see on the internet show how you move through grief like it's a straight train track, or a gentle curve making this grief thing seem so easy.

For myself, and also for my clients, my picture below is more the reality of the grief experience.

In this chapter I share grief as it really is, what you can expect today and, in the future, and the times, I believe, are the times to seek professional support.

This chapter is all based on my own professional grief guide developed from my personal and professional experiences, my studies, working with my many grief clients, of all ages, and hours upon hours of research.

It shares where you are now, where you are going, support you might need and how to plan for the future all written from someone who's been where you are now and understands the reality.

In my work supporting those grieving there is no cardboard cut-out support or process that I use for everyone because, as I've explained before, everyone grieves differently, so my professional support depends on your unique mind body link, where you are now and where you want to be in the future.

In addition, as I have a range of qualifications, these allow me to provide the most suitable support for you, if you're into alternative therapies we can use those types of methods in addition to positive psychology principles to release emotions and move forward in a positive way.

For those who like a more structured approach I can provide that too in the form of goals and exercises for you to complete.

These are just two methods I use as examples to show that you need to be sure you work with someone who provides you grief support in a way that suits you, your beliefs, values and preferences.

Grief support needs to be fluid and tailored especially for you, not ticked off the grief practitioner's checklist.

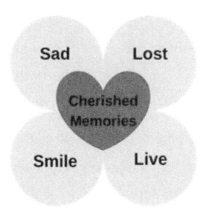

Put simply right now you are feeling sad and completely lost and where you want to be is in a better place, however that may look for you.

When I support people in their grief we focus on simple and easy steps so knowing that in the future you can and will smile and live a life with a heart full of cherished memories provides a sense of relief from the day to day turmoil and provides a small goal to understanding and looking forward to a more hopeful future.

It's really important to mention here that if you do seek support you really need to be able to have a good connection and rapport with the person you choose.

You will be sharing deeply personal moments and emotions and you need to be comfortable to do so.

If you do seek support and find you don't 'gel with the first person that's been recommended or you've chosen don't give up, support really helps when you are grieving, try another one and another if needs be.

I use a few diagrams in this chapter to explain more simply with my understanding that your mind isn't processing information as it normally does.

These diagrams came about as my clients told me that during our time together that I made the process easier to understand when I drew them my diagrams.

The Grief Flow

I found looking back after the loss of my husband and now through my studies and work with my many clients ranging in age from 12 - 89, that life after loss roughly flows into 5 Life phases.

Moving through the phases can often be an ebb and flow from one phase and then back to another.

Sometimes we can go back to a phase before again moving again.

Each phase and the time spent there will differ for everyone, as you 'take into account' your unique mind and body link including your thought processes and focus.

With each phase it must always be remembered that you do this in your own time. We, however, all start at the same place, losing a loved one and feeling grief.

The Grief Flow looks like this:

- Grief – Losing your loved one

- Reality - Realising your loved one is no longer by your side

- Interim – Not really knowing, or wanting, to move from your old life to your new life - it's like living in a dream

- Evaluate – The initial shock is wearing off, normality as you know it now begins to start in your life and you start looking forward

- Future – Looking forward and planning your future life

Each phase has many emotions entwined in them as well, of course, but broadly these are the life phases we all go through.

I can almost hear you asking me "How long does it take?"

Great question and one, I'm so sorry to say, no one can answer for you; you are uniquely you and only you will know when you start merging from one phase to another.

The worse thing about grief is that you can't delegate it to someone else, you have to get through this experience.

By arming yourself with as much information as you can and understanding the what and why's does give you more clarity and more confidence about what you will experience now and in the future.

The process of grief moves forward over time even if you 'choose' and 'will' yourself to stay in the grieving stage, life continually moves you forward as you'll see in the diagram.

You'll find that in time you'll want to move forward and yes often we move back and forth in our emotions however the process for grief usually starts with grieving, then slowly moves towards living again.

Small steps move you along the way to learning to be able to express and cope with your grief. With support of professionals, or you can do this by yourself if you choose, you slowly start to visualise a future taking small steps to create how you'll do this and then once again live your life after loss.

It all sounds simple on paper and when you read it doesn't it? Seeing the process broken down like this allows you to see each stage of the process simply and easily.

I hope you like the diagrams as they are designed to be easy to understand, not overwhelming and give a simple overview of where you are or where you'll be.

Seeking Support

Jills Reflection - *When I first saw Joy, I was in such a mess. As a woman who was quite high level at work and known to be ultra-organised and competent, I was surprised to find grief was making me so muddled. I found it hard to get dressed for work in the morning without losing half my clothes, or becoming lost in a daydream, or I'd finally go to leave and I couldn't find my phone, or keys or for that matter anything that I put down. I dreaded going to see someone for grief support as I knew if they talked at me with long winded explanations or worse still gave me exercises or stuff to do, I wouldn't be able to take anything in, I mentally and physically was tired of words.*

Seeing Joy changed all that, she totally understood where I was and shared simple diagrams and techniques I could easily understand and implement.

Looking at previous 'Grief Flow'® diagram you may find yourself asking yourself "when is the best time is to seek support from a grief specialist?

Yet again there is no straightforward answer it varies from person to person, some people like to manage alone, and others struggle from day one and need support.

Again, I stress to you that every response is normal.

I've had clients who came to see me for support a few days after the loss of their loved one to clients who came to see me years after.

In this diagram you'll see the words

- Support

- Choice

- Confidence

- Control

- Future

These five words are some of the words I use to guide you about when and why you should seek support.

I go into it in more detail below however I'll briefly give a quick overview.

When you seek support, you feel like you're being given a choice during a time when you feel like all control has gone from your life.

By choosing support and slowly taking one day at a time, with professional support you slowly gain more confidence, day by day, that you can cope, and you can get through this.

With confidence comes a spark of energy and a power to start taking control of your life once again.

Feeling able and capable enough to start looking forward and putting into action how and what your future looks like one day at a time.

My professional advice, as well as looking back to my own grief, is to seek support early, see someone for one or two appointments to talk things out, say things you feel you may feel you can't share with your family, a place where you don't have to be strong, where you won't be judged by anything you say or do, and it really clears things up and stops emotions bottling up.

You can ask questions, receive tips and techniques that will help support you in the coming days and months. Knowing someone has your back anytime really does make a difference.

It's often little things that seem so hard such as going back to work that can seem overwhelming these are some of the things a professional grief support can really assist you with.

I would then recommend you see someone either ongoing if you feel you need it, or when you start to cope a little better and need some clarity around where you're going and what you want in the future.

I have some clients who book in monthly for a phone call just to chat about things that might have cropped up over the last month, they find having that little bit of security and support helps them enormously.

I'm going to start this next piece of advice saying, I know there are plenty of amazing life coaches out there who could help you plan for the future however when you're ready to start planning I do advise and in fact highly recommend seeking out someone who specialises in grief.

Planning for the future after loss is very different to those planning a life without those layers of emotions.

Lots of emotions arise when you least expect them, and you need someone who can support you along the way with professional grief understanding and empathy.

Seeking support gives you choices and then more confidence about how you're feeling and the steps you personally need to take to bring back some sort of control in your life.

You're able to then plan, in a way that your mind can cope with, for your future whether that's for the next week, month or years ahead.

I hope these diagrams made the process, this whole grief experience, a little easier to understand and provides you information and a little more confidence that while it doesn't feel like it now things do slowly change and improve.

I know for my many clients seeing the process presented so simply gave them the information they needed about the process and outcome and is another great way to see where you are now and where you'll be in the future.

If you need support, I'm always here for you and my details can be found at the end of the book and also on the various resources I've provided in Chapter 6.

CARE & ACTIONS

Care

- Don't try and get to the end of every stage or process, it's not a race it takes time

- You may move from one stage to another and back again – it's all normal

- Seek support when you feel you need to or when others express concerns

- If you seek support and don't feel comfortable with the person try again

Actions

- Read and re read this chapter as you will align with various stages throughout your grief

- Choices give you confidence to move forward with planning

- Seek support from a grief professional instead of a life coach

CHAPTER 5: How To Cope With Loss – Healthy Ways To Manage Your Emotions

Grief can be quite lonely, and the fact is grief is one of the hardest things you'll ever have to face.

You might wonder and question if you're grieving normally, this is quite common, comparing yourself to others you've seen grieving.

My advice to you from my own experience, through my studies and supporting my clients, is to take things slowly.

Listen to your grief, your mind and body, and don't fight it, face it one small step at a time, working out what you need, not what others think you need, is crucial at this time.

In this chapter I share ways to support you to get through the early stages and some healthy ways to manage your emotions as you start to live your life without your loved one by your side.

You'll find techniques to tuck into your toolbelt, proven techniques that work when you need them throughout your day, ready to pull them out as you need to gain some control at a time when control seems to have gone out the window.

Grief comes in waves and having a few tools to help you when they hit gives you more control and reduces your anxiety about how you'll cope if and when overwhelm hits you.

If you have children the information in this chapter can be used for them as well, depending on their ages.

The Support Structure You Need

I look back now and reflect on how differently I would have walked my grief experience then but, as they say, hindsight is a wonderful thing.

I didn't know, back then, what I know now and through my own grief experiences and my professional training and work I've found ways to support people I wish I'd had access to back then.

This is why I've written this book to support you right now with ways that I have proven to will guide and support you along the way.

I truly believe support is very beneficial, and even though I chose not to seek support myself, due to me believing the myth of having to be strong, I know it would have helped me immensely.

While I've shared that everyone grieves differently, here are three of my tips I've found are essential for anyone who is grieving.

Tip One – Create A C.A.L.M® Team

One of the things I've found in my work was people's need for support from family and friends, and what I also observed was how clients would call certain people at certain times seeking specific support.

From these observations I created a way for my clients to seek and create the support structure they need I call this creating a C.A.L.M team

C.A.L.M team stands for - **Call Anytime & Listen to Me**

Your CALM team may include family, friends, leaders in your faith, a bereavement support group, and professional grief support and they provide specific support to you.

Not everyone around you can provide everything you need at this time so you'll find having people who can support you in different ways is perfect.

So, who can you add to your C.A.L.M team? You may have a favourite Aunty who makes the best cuppa and cake and she is the one you visit when you need someone to sit with as she really listens as you talk and share your feelings.

Another friend might be the one you call when you need someone who makes you laugh, a great one to add to your team.

Another C.A.L.M team member might that special someone you call when you need comfort as they give you the best hugs and don't talk at all.

Yet another might be so great at organising you call them when you feel disorganised and overwhelmed. It's good to let the people know you've added them to your C.A.L.M team as they will feel that they are supporting you in their own special way.

Tip Two - Take Good Care Of Yourself

My own short Reflection

Looking back, I realised I'd created my own C.A.L.M team when I lost my husband. I had my neighbour who I could call on while working on the extension project on our home. We chatted while we climbed ladders and in doing so, we talked about how my late husband would do things and laugh when we did it a different way.

My closest friends a beautiful family were there for me and I could drop in anytime and be welcomed with a cuppa and a chat about anything. Often, I didn't even have to talk they would fill in the whole conversation, exactly what my kids and I needed I would have been lost without them.

It can be easy to forget about our own needs when we are reeling from loss but neglecting yourself, mentally and physically won't help you as you deal with your grief.

Remember to:

- Eat small nutritional meals and if you've lost your appetite, smoothies are great to sip on and will boost you with a little energy while keeping your immunity charged.

- Sleep when you can and if you find you have broken sleep rest in the morning or afternoon even if it's only a short nap.

- Light exercise like walking is great to clear the mind and get your body moving. You'll even feel better after a walk as the endorphins and dopamine hormones are released – the feel-good hormones- helping you to lift your mood a little to assist in lifting your physical and emotional fatigue.

- Be patient with yourself and allow yourself to feel whatever your feeling.

- Understand what triggers your grief and prepare for those triggers (e.g., plan to take a day or two off of work, let your friends and family know you'll need extra support, etc.).

- Do something creative to express your feelings (e.g., write something, paint, put together a scrapbook, or play a musical instrument).

- Meditation is an awesome technique to use for calming and focus

A client's story

A client came to me desperately anxious and fearful. He explained he was unable to go shopping anymore. When I gently asked him some more questions, I found that the first time he had gone shopping he saw his wife's favourite chocolate that he's always bought as a surprise for her on a Friday night when they watched movies together. It was his little way of showing how much he cared.

On seeing the chocolate, he had automatically picked it up and placed it in his basket. When realising what he had done he was overcome with uncontrolled crying. He was fearful of, in his words, "making a fool of himself again in the shops" and "worried his family may send him to a home in case they thought he couldn't look after himself".

We started to work on some techniques and strategies together so we could turn shopping back into something he could cope with again. One of the strategies we worked on was a new routine where he would go to the shops and buy his wife's favourite chocolate and turn it into happy memories. In the end he found himself enjoying the memories of his wife as he made it a new tradition to continue watching movies every Friday night enjoying a piece of chocolate in gratitude for the times they had shared.

Tip Three - Seek Professional Grief Support

Not everyone will choose or need the services of a professional for support during grief, but it can be very helpful.

A qualified professional can help you understand the grief process and provide you with tools and techniques you can use to cope with your emotions.

I've had many clients say to me they wish they had come to see me sooner rather than later as they found instant ease in gaining control through the tips and techniques I shared.

The Firsts & How To Deal With Them

There will be many firsts, more than you realise, you'll face within the first year following the loss of your loved one.

Some like birthdays, anniversaries are firsts you'll be expecting.

There are other firsts that came when I least expected them, the first date of when we had met, the first time I received a letter addressed to my husband or hearing his favourite song blaring from the radio.

Other firsts maybe attending an event for the first time alone such as family celebrations or friends get together, 'making a decision' that normally you'd make with your loved one, all these firsts are also hard.

Planning and being prepared for firsts are the best way to deal with them.

For example, for your the first anniversary of the loss of your loved one plan to go to the cemetery or your special place the day before instead of on the day.

That way you can then plan to be alone on the actual day or spend it quietly with family or friends or even, if you choose too, shut yourself away for a day of remembering the good times and acknowledging your feelings in private.

It's important to share with family what you plan to do, or they may feel they'll have to plan something for you.

How To Respond To Other Peoples Comments & Reactions

Only a small percentage of advice given to you is actually helpful right now and 'well-intentioned' advice is one of the hardest things to deal with, as is the often-confusing reactions of others.

Advice and comments can often trigger responses in you that surprise you and can leave you breathless and wondering if what they have uttered has really been said out of love.

The most important thing to remember is, as I've mentioned before, is that people who have never grieved simply don't understand.

Being forewarned and prepared is the best tool so here below is a list of some of the comments you may find shared with you.

"I know how you feel." Grief is unique for everyone. Even if we have had a similar loss in our own life, we really have no idea how someone is really feeling. They would be better off saying, "I can relate to your loss," instead of "I know how you feel."

"Be strong." Telling someone to be strong is actually asking you to hide your grief. This is one of the worst messages we can give. Emotions are what make us human. They also help with the healing process. Showing emotions is especially important if there are any children involved.

Children need to see it's okay to have, and to express, both happy and sad emotions.

"At least they aren't suffering anymore." If a loved one died of a long-term illness, it's probably true that their suffering is over. However, it doesn't change the fact that we still feel heartbroken by the loss. Even though the person may be able to rationalize this statement in their head, saying it doesn't help our heart to feel any better.

"Be grateful for the time you had together." We are all grateful for the time we had with a loved one. However, this particular statement may make you feel they you shouldn't feel sad about their loss. In reality, it's okay to be both grateful for the time spent with someone and sad over losing them.

"Everything happens for a reason." Saying this to you may or may not be true depending on your spiritual beliefs. Even if it is spiritually true, it's

another statement that won't help our heart feel any better. It's once again like making their loss seem insignificant as if you shouldn't grieve because it was their time to go end of story.

"Just give it time." Wouldn't it be nice if grief had a time limit? Unfortunately, it doesn't. Even if we experienced a loved one's death a long time ago, we can still feel the sadness and grief today. Although we may be able to cope better with the death after a period of time, we never get over the loss. By saying this statement to someone who is grieving is implying that with time our heartbreak will get better and we'll forget. We can heal, we can start living our life again but the loss we feel now will always be there, it will become a part of our DNA and we will find we will remember with smiles and not so many tears. However, time does not make you forget them.

What To Do When Overwhelm Hits You

Overwhelmed with grief?

It is entirely normal to feel overwhelmed with grief, it is a natural and human response to loss.

To understand why overwhelm and all the confusion and feeling of helplessness that comes with it we need to understand a little about how our brains function.

Our brains create pathways every time we do something and the more, we do something the easier it is for the brain to travel along this pathway without you even thinking about it.

To better understand this, think back to when you were learning to drive.

You'd never driven before so your brain didn't know what it was doing, it had to concentrate, to focus, you couldn't cope well with distractions because you were focusing so much on learning.

Your brain processes grief in the same way it processes anything new, just like driving a car.

Every time you had a driving lesson, every time you got behind the wheel your brain was creating a pathway known as the neural pathway.

The more you drove the deeper the neural pathway became until you could drive and talk at the same time, you could drive without much concentration at all.

Today you most probably get the car keys out now you don't even have to think about driving, the brain associates those keys with driving, and it knows what to do, it becomes automatic.

Now you probably drive from A to B and not even remember much of the trip at all.

Grieving is the same, your brain doesn't understand it, it doesn't know how to respond there isn't a pathway for it to follow so it becomes confused and overwhelmed.

It knows your reaction to sadness, however as grief is a new deeper sadness response it is just like learning to drive, the brain needs to create a new pathway.

This is why you feel tired, and foggy your mind is trying to focus in on where it needs to go and cope with where it is now.

Mindfulness

Mindfulness is a fantastic technique to support you through grief Mindfulness simply means 'Noticing your emotions without judgement' and is great way of noticing how you're feeling and acknowledging those emotions.

Giving yourself permission in a given moment to go "you know I feel sad, I feel overwhelmed and that's ok I have every right to feel this way".

By acknowledging your emotions, you take away any judgement and your mind can then go "ok I recognise I feel sad I know that feeling I know I need to cry, and it feels a little better".

This is a really simplified description of mindfulness however, mindfulness is a very effective method for grief.

Grief Retreats

A retreat that nurtures and supports you is also a useful way to heal away from well-meaning family and friends and gives you the chance to take back some control of your life, breathe and find yourself some understanding of grief.

You'll learn methods and techniques that will assist you in the coming days. Group support, for grief can also support you as you often find comfort in sharing with others going through grief the same as you are.

If you're wary of going to a grief retreat thinking it will be sad and miserable most are not.

I run grief retreats and they are not sombre, sad and miserable like most people associate grief retreats with, my own retreats are all based on positive gentle support.

For example, on my grief retreats you are nurtured, cared for, provided with tips and techniques, strategies and most of all support.

You have time to be alone or time with others it's all self-paced for you and you alone. When you're grieving you often don't feel like eating and the thought of preparing food often puts you off entirely that's where a grief retreat is also great.

On my retreats I cater for you, so you don't need to think about shopping, preparing and eating, you simply turn up and the nourishing food is ready when you are.

Janes Reflection On Attending A Grief Retreat - *After the loss of my husband I felt like I was suffocating under the love and sympathy from my family and friends. Sounds strange doesn't it that I was so cared for and loved but instead of the support I thought it would give me I found it way too much! I found that I became increasingly desperate to be alone and escape and that's when I found Joys (Mind Body Joy) nurturing retreat especially for those grieving. I arrived at her retreat place and immediately felt at ease, Joy seemed to instinctively know when I needed space and when I needed a hug. She shared information about why I felt the way I did, and I found that having it explained to me took away some of the angst I felt about crying all the time. I was also provided with nourishing and healthy food which certainly helped as my appetite hadn't been good at all and I found that eating small and regular meals certainly helped boost my energy and physically strengthened me as well.*

The techniques she provided have been a lifesaver I remember once I was in the supermarket and I felt anxious and panic rising in my chest. I immediately stopped and used my favourite tool that Joy had taught me, the '3 Minute to Calm' method, and the anxiety and panic abated.

I had felt such guilt going away and having time by myself but having the support at Joys grief retreat was the best choice I ever made. I highly recommend it for anyone experiencing grief it really helped me and I know it will help you too.

Seek Support

Seeking support from trained grief professionals is also a great way to support you if you are feeling overwhelmed.

Grief professionals understand and can provide support to you in ways such as listening, mindful methods, meditation and other techniques to support you.

I highly recommend seeking support early, when you are supported by someone who listens, who will work with you on what methods will work best for you and your personal overwhelm.

Seeking support will give you back some control in your life at a time when it feels like you are in a vortex being pulled in so many directions.

Remember the longer you stay in deep grief and the emotions around that your brain is making new pathways and often this is where people get stuck.

It's important to remember different methods and support will work for different people.

Put A Plan In Place

Putting a plan in place with simple goals with what you want to do today, and tomorrow is a start to gaining back a feeling that you aren't spinning madly out of control.

Making small plans, ones the brain can focus on without too much effort, reduces overwhelm by bringing back some form of control during a time when everything feels so totally out of your control. There's no time period for grief.

Grief is different for everyone, grief never really goes away it becomes a part of you, it's what you do and how you adjust and work with it that is most important.

There are many ways to cope with grief with quite a few suggestions above for you to choose from.

My biggest tip is to find something you like to do. Don't join a large grief support group if you are an introvert for instance. If you can't stand writing, then don't start a journal for the sake of hearing that it helps some people. Remember as I say throughout this book your grief is personal, you will find ways that suit you and support you in your everyday.

CARE & ACTIONS

Care

- Do what you intuitively know you need to de-stress and cope with all around you

- Take your time in everything you do

- Spoil yourself with time doing things you love

Actions

- Create your C.A.L.M team

- Try new things to relax like meditation, yoga or joining a walking group

- Look for a support group if you prefer social support

- Look for grief retreats

CHAPTER 6: Moving Forward

– A New Normal

The weirdest thing with grief is that life continues to move on around you.

Your whole world has exploded and changed, and yet you go to the shops and everything is still the same, how can the world keep turning?

I see in my clients, and also when I lost my husband, the struggle to let go of the life I loved living with my husband.

I feared being seen to be moving forward would be seen as forgetting him in some way.

I also had my young children to think about, if life got to a new normal quickly would they think we had already moved on and Dad would be forgotten?

It's hard when you've lost your loved one and you have to move into a new life without them by your side.

Moving forward is like a swing, you fear if you move forward, you're letting go of another piece of your heart and the memories.

You fear letting go the love you still rightly feel of your loved one to knowing that you have to move forward and start a life without them by your side.

Back and forth up and down like a swing your emotions go; it's no wonder w feel so unbalanced and overwhelmed.

There is one important thing you need to know right here and now and that is planning and building a new life does not mean you forget your loved one, it means that those memories can be cherished and talked about and always there in your heart no matter where you go from here.

The old saying of they wouldn't want you to live the rest of your life in sadness really is true. My whole philosophy in life and particularly in grief and loss is to look back on the life you shared with love and happiness, not sadness.

In saying that of course you'll feel sad, I still do all these years later, however if you hold the precious memories with gratitude for the time you had together, remember the laughs, the funny inside jokes and family traditions it makes everything seem a tiny bit more easier and it makes their life worth living.

When you remember with gratitude, happiness and love you are honouring their time with you and the love you shared.

Being By Yourself

Being by yourself is also very personal to each and every one of us.

Again, how your relationships were with your loved one will also influence how you cope with being by yourself now they are no longer by your side.

If you spent nearly all your hours together you will find being by yourself very hard to adjust to. If you had independent lives it may be easier to adjust to, there's just no telling how you'll react.

I found he hardest time for me was being alone was at night lying in bed with his empty pillow beside me where his head should be resting.

I'd loved our night chats, where my husband and I would talk about our day, our kids and various other topics. Without him by me at night, his empty pillow beside me was the toughest of being alone.

You share so much with your loved one, things no one else would ever know, the real side of you, and that's what I found the hardest of being all alone.

Also, as a family, my husband and I spent all our spare time together, we loved family time together and our holidays were always together, we never holidayed alone.

Holidays were going to be very different now he was gone. As mentioned previously as soon as the funeral and legal stuff was over, I took the kids away, away to our happy place where we had holidayed many, many times.

We had time away from people and it was the first step in our new life without their Dad, and my husband.

My advice for being by yourself is like all the advice in this book, take it slowly. It's hard to adjust to a totally new life especially when you don't want to adjust to it at all.

Be realistic and take it one step at a time, one day at a time and then when you feel less overwhelmed start with one week at a time and so on.

Choose someone from your C.A.L.M team to support you. Maybe one of your team would be great to meet up with you after you go to the movies by yourself for the first time.

By having plans in place and support ready for you you'll feel more in control and ready to take the step.

Your first holiday might be as a group holiday so you still have people around, or you may choose a weekend away and ease into now having holidays by yourself.

Look at the plans you may have had for the future that you and your loved one were planning to do. Maybe as a way to cherish and honour their memory you could plan to do some of them in the future.

Designing Your New Life

Designing your life sounds exciting and glamourous doesn't it?

In reality it can be hard, and it can be exciting as well.

You might find that plans your loved one and yourself had talked about are now particularly relevant such as downsizing your family home, travelling or even selling a car.

As I mentioned in chapter two please don't make huge life decisions in the early days of losing your loved one, in fact I advise all my clients not to consider major changes or decisions for at least twelve months or even more.

When thinking about your new life look at how you can keep emotionally connected to your relationship with your loved one now, they aren't with you physically.

Make the memories and connection beautiful, such as compiling a play list of their favourite songs, or planting a special rose or their plant they loved in their memory so that every time it blooms you think of them

The other thing to consider when you are looking at your new is that you now need to find your own place in the world.

You may find that your identity was intrinsically linked with your loved one. Did you love being Fred's wife and most people associated you in that way?

Or were you known as Sally's husband again finding yourself linked?

Being known as yourself is often hard when you loved your identity linked with your loved one and finding yourself being introduced in a new way is often hard at first.

Create a new ornament for your Christmas tree or to place on the table for family events in memory of your loved one, there are lots of ways to keep the connection special.

Clients Story - *A client came to me worried about the first Christmas spent without her Mum. She was really worried as the whole family were not coping very well and she was worried a day that was so loved and so special in the past by her Mum would now be spoilt. She understood their sadness but knew her Mum wouldn't want the day spoiled by tears and made sad forever more. She was desperate to make it special but was at a loss of what to do*

As we had spoken about her Mums love of craft, I suggested to her that she buy some clear plastic bauble and raid her Mums craft cupboard and on Christmas day get everyone to create a special bauble in memory of their Mum/Nan and Wife. By doing an activity together it started conversations about her Mum and her love of craft and also bought laughter as they discussed how she would have made a very special bauble.

Simple things like this bring people together and create new memories, now every Christmas they pull out those baubles in memory of their Mum

How do you design a new life?

You need to start with a plan and that can be quite overwhelming so my tip is to start by writing down everything you can think of, it doesn't have to make sense right now and you don't need the answer right now either, just get it down on paper.

Write it simply and easily in dot points for example it may look like this

- Cars

- House

- Work

- Holidays

- Clothes to donate

- What do I want to do with my life now?

- Health

- Movies

- Group events

- Friends gatherings

- Firsts

- House maintenance

- Things my loved one did, can I do them or do
  I need to organise some help

- Finances

The above is a sample only, once thing I found when I lost my husband was that the whipper snipper, a petrol one had to have certain adjustments to get it started.

I can tell you that that whipper snipper became the bane of my life as I pulled and pulled the line to start it to no avail.

It wasn't until I asked one of my C.A.L.M support that I was told you need to switch on more petrol to start it and of course when they did that it started first time!

Small things like this are what you should add to your list as in the early stages of grief when you think you're finally holding things together overwhelm and frustration can hit like a tonne of bricks like it did with the whipper snipper. I found myself wondering if I'd ever be able to cope without my love.

Set yourself some goals once you've created your list however, I'm going to stress yet again make the goals short term and very flexible.

The less pressure you put on yourself the better.

Go through your list and sort them into priority of what you want to do and have to do for your future life.

Talk to your C.A.L.M team seek support from them as you work your way through things.

Know that moving on with your life into a new normal life without the one you love doesn't mean your forgetting them, they will always be in your heart and no one or nothing can ever take that away.

Moving on doesn't mean you forget it means that your living continues until you meet again.

While this book has provided basic information, it is provided as a guide for you in the beginning. There is more depth that I could go into and will do so in an upcoming book.

I'll finish now in summary to say I'm so sorry for your loss of your love, I feel your pain and truly wish I could give you a hug through these pages.

I hope I have given and provided you some support, love and understanding in these days of your grief and I wish you all the best for the future.

I end as I always do say "We are making memories today for tomorrow, make them good ones" and "always fill everyday with Joy".

CARE & ACTIONS

Care

- Don't try and do everything at once

- You don't need to design a brand-new life if you only need to tweak your old one

- Take the support of others

Actions

- Write down everything that's worrying you

- Create a plan from that worry list

- Set short term and flexible goals

- Adjust your goals if you need too

- Find ways to connect emotionally with your loved one by creating special items or listening to their favourite songs

- Seek support from a professional if it all gets too much or you need guidance

CHAPTER 7: Tools & Techniques To Support You Now And In the Future

So, we have reached the end of the book and as you know I've mentioned care and action points along the way.

In this chapter I provide you with various tools and techniques to help you along the way all in simple easy to read ways. In here you'll find checklists and techniques to help you every day and I have provided these free as my gift to you.

Throughout the book I mention all the legal and other things you need to do after the loss of your loved one.

To make it easier for you I have compiled a collection of checklists to assist and guide you through the first few moments, hours and weeks after the loss of your loved one.

Each checklist is simple and easy to read and will reduce the overwhelm of all the legal and other things you need to do after the loss of your loved one.

I have also included in this chapter techniques I have created specifically to assist with grief which will support you when the overwhelm hits.

Of course, as your mind won't be capable of taking in much information all techniques are quick and easy to learn.

To access the checklist and techniques please go to my website https://mindbodyjoy.com.au/book-bonuses/

where you'll be able to download everything and print them ready for when you need them.

CHECKLISTS

Time of Loss and Onwards Checklist

This checklist provides you with everything you need to do in those first few moments, hours and weeks after the loss of your loved one, one step at a time

Farewell Planning Checklist

This checklist supports you to plan the farewell of your loved one. To be used as a guide only as it helps you make decisions about whether you want a burial or cremation, funeral or memorial and so on.

Journaling

My Silent Moments is a beautiful and nurturing way to recall those cherished moments after the loss of your loved one. If you print out double sided copies of this, you can create your own journal of cherished memories.

TECHNIQUES

3 Minutes to Calm®

I created this simple and effective technique to control overwhelm fast, within in three minutes in fact. This is a simple and easy technique to learn that will support you in those situations where you feel the overwhelm hit you like a tonne of bricks

Mind Body Joy Open Eye meditation

I designed this little open eye meditation to load onto your phone specifically for those moments when your brain won't stop and the overwhelm hits you, it's also perfect to support you to fall asleep. You simply watch and listen and that's it, no thinking and nothing to learn. This meditation is designed to be listened to with headphones or earbuds.

I hope you find these checklists and techniques useful my clients love them. I also provide more useful resources on my website so make sure you check them out too, most are free as I truly believe no one should be left in overwhelm every day.

I would love to hear from you so please feel free to reach out via email, joy@mindbodyjoy.com.au, your feedback is important for my future books.

So together we finish our time together, however this book is not meant to be closed forever, use it as a reference for when you feel overwhelmed, you're in need of answers to question and most of all to be your guiding support for today and tomorrow.

I'll end as I always do saying:

"We are making tomorrows memories today so make them good ones and always remember to Fill Everyday with Joy".

With Love

Joy

About The Author

Joy Fairhall – Connecting Mind, Body and Joy

When life throws you a curveball, Joy Fairhall is the person you want in your corner.

As the founder of Mind Body Joy, she brings personal insight and professional expertise to help overcome and manage a life-changing event.

Joy has a specialist interest in people dealing with fear and overwhelm after the loss of their loved one. And her insight comes from a uniquely personal place.

"I began my journey to learn more about the mind and body and joy over 23 years ago when my husband passed away quite suddenly when I was 37 and my children were 12 and 14," Joy explains.

"That moment changed our lives forever. I was lost and sought to understand the depth of my grief and found that the topic of death and grief was not openly discussed and books at that time were limited on the topic.

Since that time, I have researched, studied and qualified in many areas of health and wellness modalities with my focus always on finding ways to support people lost in the turmoil of grief.

Joy shares and explains grief in a way that is uniquely real, right from the very moment you lose your loved one.

She believes that understanding your reactions and feelings from those first moments, weeks months and years makes the whole experience a bit less overwhelming and gives you back some control in your life at a time when you feel like life will never be normal ever again.

Her unique understanding, through her own experience and her work with her many clients as well as her studies and research, has provided her with an insight other don't have and this has led her to develop her own way of sharing the reality of grief.

Her grief overview is designed in such a way that is simple and easy to read and understand.

The diagrams she uses to show what you can expect came about as a direct result from her own grief experience and understanding, that reading too much information is simply impossible in the early stages of grief.

"I have seen so many client's lives changed when they understand grief and they are given simple, easy and effective tools and techniques to support them along the way from someone who's been where they are now" says Joy.

Her unique understanding gives you comfort in knowing she shares the reality of grief as it really is.

As a warm, committed and nurturing professional with proven results, her clients range from tweens to seniors. Joy supports them to cope, understand and to know there is a future ready continually supporting them to take the next step in life.

As a sought-after speaker Joy brings her vast range of skills, expertise and her own personal life experiences to connect, support and guide with every audience enabling them to understand their unique Mind and Body and Joy link.

Her connection to the audience, no matter the size, feels intimate and nurturing, she will make them laugh, sometimes cry and always connect to themselves creating ah ha moments in a way that is truly unique.

Joy Fairhall - Ph. 0439 564 385,

Email - joy@mindbodyjoy.com.au

Website - www.mindbodyjoy.com.au

Facebook - https://www.facebook.com/mindbodyjoy/

LinkedIn – https://www.linkedin.com/in/joyfairhall/

Twitter- https://twitter.com/JoyMindBodyJoy